# YOU
# SAY

DISCOVERING GOD'S PLAN FOR
OUR COMMUNICATION

## RYAN BISEL, Ph.D.

WESTBOW
P R E S S®
A DIVISION OF THOMAS NELSON
& ZONDERVAN

WestBow Press books may be ordered through booksellers or by contacting:

WestBow Press
A Division of Thomas Nelson & Zondervan
1663 Liberty Drive
Bloomington, IN 47403
www.westbowpress.com
1 (866) 928-1240

ISBN: 978-1-5127-3523-9 (sc)
ISBN: 978-1-5127-3524-6 (e)

Print information available on the last page.

WestBow Press rev. date: 4/4/2016

*Dedicated to Dorothy, Dee, Julie (2 Tim 1:5),*
*and my dearest Adele (P&D!)*

*Who open their mouths with wisdom,*
*and teach kindness (Prov. 31:26)*

The author would like to thank Katherine M. Kelley and Stacie Wilson Mumpower for their helpful comments on earlier versions of this work.

# CONTENTS

# CHAPTER 1

# God's Plan for our Communication

"God spoke about how we speak. He commented on our commenting," I said to myself as I stared at a passage in Malachi, blinking, then smiling, then feeling a chill of sorrowful clarity that is sometimes attained by reading God's Word in a new way.

While I am not proud of it, I must admit the day I realized this truth I was "angry-reading" the Bible. Have you ever done that? I was reading Malachi for it's famous passages about tithing and God's provision for those who tithe faithfully. Why was I angry? I need to take you back: My wife and I—on the strong recommendation from most everyone we trusted—bought a little, aging home in a college town. The standard advice was: "Just get into the market however you can. It's the best investment. In a few years you can use the equity generated here to afford to make a down payment on a home you really want." So we bought a home in 2004. In 2008, we were ready to sell the home after God provided a career opportunity in another state.

To us, every aspect of the career opportunity was a Godsend. We felt loved and nurtured. We felt affirmed. Every conceivable obstacle seemed to dissolve before us and a great future seemed in sight. However, when we went to sell our little house during the summer of 2008—yeah, 2008, the peak of the Great Recession—there were no takers, not even lookers. We rented eventually and felt a sense of relief; the outcome was not ideal according to us, but we thanked God anyway. In our unfortunate and earthly wisdom, we decided to try again in the summer of 2010. "Surely the house will sell now," we thought. It didn't. For ten long months, we could neither sell the house nor rent it successfully. For ten months, we struggled to pay two mortgages. I prayed. I fasted. I bargained. I felt betrayed. I questioned myself. I sought out Godly advice. We wondered whether we were being punished. That's when I was rereading the passages in Malachi about tithing and God's blessing. "We tithe," I thought. "Were is our 'overflowing blessing (Mal. 3:10)?'" As my eyes continued to read the passages that followed, my veins ran cold.

> You have spoken harsh words against me, says the LORD. Yet *you say*, 'How have we spoken against you?' *You have said*, "It is vain to serve God. What do we profit by keeping his command or by going about as

> mourners before the LORD of hosts? Now
> we count the arrogant happy; evildoers not
> only prosper, but when they put God to the
> test they escape (Mal. 3:13-15).

"*You say*," I repeated to myself aloud. The Holy Spirit convicted me. Whether I spoke it aloud, or to myself, I knew I had not honored God with my words. I honored God with my tithe, but then, when the circumstances of life did not unfold as I expected, I grumbled. I looked at what others—who do not know the LORD—seemed to enjoy and I was bitter. Yes, I coveted. I asked forgiveness and God provided, as He always does. That moment put a fire in my spirit to learn more about what God wants from my words. I wanted to know more about God—not my idea of God, but who God really is. Now, knowing Him more, we receive blessing, which no amount of money can buy. Today, many years later, I do not believe God was punishing us. Quite the opposite, I believe he was wooing us to dig deeper, to discover a special revealing of Himself.

Read in its entirety, the book of Malachi has much to say about how we fail to honor God with our words. Consider, Malachi 2:17:

> You have wearied the LORD with your
> words. Yet *you say*, "How have we wearied
> Him?" By saying, "All who do evil are good
> in the sight of the LORD and he delights
> in them." Or by asking, "Where is the God
> of justice?

How often must we weary the LORD with our words? Do we pay our sacrifices of time, talent, and treasure, without giving thought to our tongue—the quality of our words and how those words honor or dishonor Him? Perhaps, like me, your first impression is, "C'mon, really? Now I need to think about everything I *say*?" Notice, in the passage above, the LORD knows the audience will react with irritation and gall to the accusation that their everyday talk wearies Him. The LORD knows the audience will react by questioning, "How have we wearied Him?" What is your response to the idea that the LORD desires us to investigate our words carefully? Does the task appear so difficult or trivial that it is not worth pursuing? But, there is hope. Near the end of the book of Malachi, the author concludes, "Then those who revered the LORD *spoke* with one another. The LORD took note and *listened*, and a book of remembrance was written before him of those who revered the LORD and thought on his name" (Mal. 3:16). May it be with us.

"*You say*," are two little words. They are so seemingly insignificant I wonder how many times we read them without giving much thought to their importance. In these passages, those words indicate God is about to discuss our discussion, describe our descriptions, and talk about the quality of our talk!

I needed to know more. I wondered what other lessons God had in store. To that end, I undertook to study as many situations in the Bible as possible, which included some variation of the phrase, "*You say*," and constituted God's (be it Jesus, Prophets, or Apostles speaking on God's behalf) commenting on our commenting. Depending on the translation, I discovered there are a little more than 100 such instances throughout the pages of Scripture. I do not mean to suggest my list is exhaustive, but I did review these passages with great care and close scrutiny. While I am no biblical scholar, I am a communication scholar and a social scientist. My training helped me to notice the importance of such tiny words like, "*You say.*" When I was a doctoral student in communication, I learned that when interview participants began a sentence with, "And then *he said . . .,*" I needed to pay attention because whatever followed was an account of someone's communication.

My process of investigating these passages was to read and reread each in context. As you can imagine, the process took many months. I moved back and forth among these passages attempting to locate unifying themes or lessons. The task was difficult because at first blush the instances in which "*You say*" arises in the Bible seemed much too diverse to have any commonality. Some passages are extended texts; others are a few words in length. Some passages are about the future; others are about the past or present. Some passages are narrative and historical, others are proverbial, while others are primarily theological. In the end, through much prayer and study, a unifying perspective came into focus. In the following pages, I explain what I learned through this process of discovery about God's plan for biblical communication. The book unfolds in two main sections. In the first section, I describe some surprising (even counterintuitive) insights the Bible teaches about the nature of communication itself. This study has emphasized for me how much more complex the Bible's teaching on communication is than merely being "nice." In the second section, I outline the primary unifying theme of my in-depth study of biblical communication.

---

## Discussion Questions, Chapter 1

1. Look again at the passages in Malachi mentioned in this chapter. What do these passages suggest about God's view of our talk?
2. Which falsehood would you be more tempted to believe: Studying communication is too difficult or too trivial? Why?
3. Tell your story of a time when you failed to honor God with your words.

# CHAPTER 2

# **Talk is action**

"Talk is cheap" and "Actions speak louder than words" are common sayings in our culture. The sayings are not without merit. Proverbs 14:23 reads, "In all toil there is profit, but mere talk leads only to poverty." Almost certainly there are instances in which talk can be cheap. There are times when actions demonstrate our own and others' real intentions much more than empty promises and hollow commitments. However, these sayings might hide the fact that words *are* actions and talk *can be costly*. Consider the following passages:

> And whatever you do, in *word* or deed, do everything in the name of the LORD Jesus, giving thanks to God the Father through him (Col. 3:17).

> Death and life are in the power of the
> tongue, and those who love it will eat its
> fruits (Prov. 18:21).

In the first passage, Paul includes a clause to ensure we understand that "doing" includes the speaking of words. Likewise, in the second passage, Solomon provides a surprising, but wise, insight: The power of the tongue is an issue of life and death! When we think of these ideas together, we realize that talk is action of grave importance. Having a hard time seeing how talk could be important? Consider walking into an elevator—which amounts to a steal cage— with a National Football League (NFL) middle linebacker. Would you insult his mother or his performance at last Sunday's game? Of course, acting that way is not only rude, but it also may have very "physical" consequences. Have you ever been the victim of gossip or a broken promise? These too are obvious ways in which speaking is action—actions that can result in hurt, not only physically, but emotionally and relationally as well.

## Talk can be sin (or a Godly work).

For many believers, to say talk can be a sin is probably not hard to believe. The Ten Commandments provides an explicit admonition against certain kinds of speech: "You shall not make wrongful use of the name of the LORD your God, for the LORD will not acquit anyone who misuses his name" (Ex. 20:7) and "Do not bear false witness" (Ex. 20:16). Yet, on first examination, few other commandments appear to deal directly with the nature of sinful talk. Without

question, blasphemy and false witness are sinful examples
of talk. However, during the Sermon on the Mount, Jesus
himself teaches us to read the Commandments more fully,
to include the role of talk at nearly every turn.

> Again you have heard that it was said to
> those of ancient times, 'You shall not swear
> falsely, but carry out the vows you have
> made to the LORD.' But I say to you, Do
> not swear at all, either by heaven, for it is
> the throne of God, or by the earth, for it is
> his footstool, or by Jerusalem, for it is the
> city of the great King. And do not swear by
> your head, for you cannot make one hair
> white or black. Let your word be 'Yes, Yes'
> or 'No, No;' anything more than this comes
> from the evil one (Mt. 5:33-37).

Jesus reveals how the Commandment against bearing false
witness is not only confined to making deceptive accusations
against others in court (i.e., perjury). The commandment
against false witness includes the kinds of everyday talk,
commitments, promises, and business deals, which so often
present themselves alongside swearing, oaths, and contracts.

Specifically, Jesus is teaching us to reject the insertion of
language between our intentions *and what we say about* our
intentions. Notice there is no gap between yes and no (i.e.,
Let your word be "Yes, Yes" or "No, No"). What is intended
about the future is what is communicated about the future:
If I wish to agree to a pact, I agree; if I wish to refrain from
giving my commitment, I refrain. How tempting it is to

create verbiage—both written and verbally—to disguise our true intentions. With this admonition, Jesus calls any language we would seek to add between our intentions and what we say about our intentions, "from the evil one." That is not to say that we cannot be polite. The crucial point concerns whether we are falsely shaping how others understand our intentions or beliefs while also disregarding or even harming others' genuine interests.

Where others' genuine interests are involved, are you representing your intentions authentically when you communicate? Flattery is a great example of the difficulty of following Jesus' teaching. Complimenting and inflating others' perception of themselves ingratiates them to us and wins social capital. Many find it useful for winning influence in their church, home, and workplace. However, flattery creates a scenario in which others' genuine interests are disregarded because it sets them up for future failure (compare with Prov. 29:5). Why is it so tempting to engage in flattery then? Flattery wins friends in the short term, but is not true friendship (compare with Prov. 27:6).

## Talk that appears to be sinful can nonetheless be righteous.

During the Sermon on the Mount, Jesus teaches a radically expanded view of the Ten Commandments—one that includes a view of our actions taken with our words as *integral* to obeying God's law. Consider, for example, another place at which Jesus reveals our deficient perspective on the Ten Commandments:

> You have heard that is was said to those of ancient times, 'You shall not murder;' and 'whoever murders shall be liable to judgment.' But I say to you that if you are angry with a brother or sister, you will be liable to judgment; and if you insult a brother or sister you will be liable to the council; and if *you say*, 'You fool,' you will be liable to the hell of fire (Mt. 5:21-22).

Jesus reveals how the Commandment against murder is not only confined to the taking of life but also applies to the very words we use. Difficult, huh? The Commandment against murder includes those mental and communicative actions that seek to destroy or diminish others. Tough teaching, isn't it? Have you called another a fool? Have you called others worse than a fool? I have. What I hope to make clear, however, is that Jesus' teaching is not merely an admonition to be nice. He is emphasizing a courtroom metaphor by repeating the word, *liable*—a word that connotes being subject to oversight by a ruling authority. Read the passage again carefully and you will notice Jesus does not teach that saying the words, "You fool," will necessarily result in a sentence to hell. He tells us that such language will make us *liable*—that is, subject to oversight by God. In other words, we will have to give an account to Him for how we use our words in regards to others.

## You brood of vipers.

Jesus talked often about talk. On one such occasion, Jesus healed a man who was blind and mute. The book of Matthew records the "crowds were amazed and said, 'Can this be the Son of David'" (Mt. 12:23)? Perhaps motivated by jealousy, the Pharisees—a powerful religious group—described Jesus' healing powers as created "by Beelzebub" (Mt. 12:24). In other words, the Pharisees choose to make sense of Jesus' healing ability as coming from satanic power, not from God. More than that, the Pharisees, because of their high status, maintained much influence over how common folks understood the meaning of religious events. Matthew then records that Jesus "knew what they [the Pharisees] were thinking" (Mt. 12:25) and provides an extended teaching that culminates with the following words about words:

> Either make the tree good, and its fruit good; or make the tree bad, and its fruit bad; for the tree is known by its fruit. You brood of vipers! How can you speak good things, when you are evil? For out of the abundance of the heart the mouth speaks. The good person brings good things out of a good treasure. I tell you, on the day of judgment you will have to give an account for every careless word you utter; for by your words you will be justified, and by your words you will be condemned (Mt. 12:33-37)

Here, Jesus uses the metaphor of a fruit tree to describe the sinful talk of the Pharisees. In that metaphor, the tree is the corrupted sin-nature of the Pharisees (and us!) and its fruit corresponds to the illegitimate way the Pharisees spoke about Jesus' miracle—speech that selected a self-serving interpretation and tried to get others to pick up and agree with that interpretation (i.e., Jesus was working by Satan's power and not God's). Their interpretation is self-serving in the sense that it maintained their own religious authority by questioning Jesus' authority. The Pharisees' speech here was particularly heinous because their words could have caused some to attribute the wrong meaning to Jesus' healing powers and even led them to miss the opportunity to know and experience Christ. Talk of that sort is truly a sin, indeed.

Did you catch that Christ describes the Pharisees as a brood of vipers? In other words, he called the Pharisees the offspring of snakes. Great commentaries are available on the potentially multiple meanings of this phrase in its original cultural context; however, I want to direct your attention back. Remember, Jesus taught, "if *you say*, 'You fool,' you will be liable to the hell of fire" (Mt. 5:22). Describing a group as the offspring of snakes seems to be at least equivalent to the idea of calling another a fool. But these two passages inform one another when laid side-by-side and Scripture helps us interpret Scripture. Jesus' purpose here was to engage in moral teaching—not only for the Pharisees but also for the crowd of common folk who might be easily influenced by the Pharisees who were religious authorities.

What both passages have in common is their emphasis, not on specific words per se, but on the idea that we will be *liable* (i.e., subject to oversight by a higher authority; Mt. 5:22) for every *careless* word we speak (Mt. 12:36). On deeper reflection, it is clear that Jesus' words in both passages were "full-of-care" (i.e., the opposite of "careless"). His words were careful in the sense that he selected each word carefully but also in the sense that he ultimately was being caring for his audiences because eternal inheritances were at stake. The idea that we will "give an account for every careless word" (Mt. 12:37) makes me shiver and a little short of breath. How often do we speak without selecting our words carefully and without thinking about how our words provide care to others?

On a deeper level, laying these passages side-by-side also reveals that we should reject a view of Godly speech as being talk that is merely polite or nice. Jesus was not polite to the Pharisees, but his words were caring at every point. Take a look back: God's plan for Godly speech is far deeper and more complex than merely being nice. Manners and politeness are no doubt very important and often embodies much of what God wants from his people's behavior. Likewise, avoiding profanity used as a means of demeaning others is no doubt important. However, God's plan for our communication is one that requires care—careful selection of words, genuine care for others, and care in thinking about this complex teaching. Sometimes—as with Jesus' rebuke of the Pharisees in front of the crowd—to care *is* to confront.

## Discussion Questions, Chapter 2

1. Tell your story of a situation that illustrates how talk can be action of great importance.

2. Knowing that you will be liable—that is, subject to God's oversight—for every "careless" word, identify the *times* and *places* you seem to be most likely to speak carelessly.

3. How do these passages expand your notion of Godly communication beyond merely being nice?

# CHAPTER 3

# Talk-Belief-Sin

Communication is a behavior. More than that, communication is a special category of behavior. Why? Communication is the behavior that gives behavior value or meaning. Take, for example, the behavior of running. Running requires rapid movement of the legs and requires the coordination of a number of physiological systems like the circulatory, respiratory, and nervous systems. What we do not and cannot know is why a person runs without the behavior of communication. Is a runner exercising or escaping? Is exercise praiseworthy or preposterous? Is escaping devious or defying danger? Communication is the behavior that imbues behavior with value and meaning and helps us to answer these kinds of questions about most every matter large and small. Communication helps us make sense of the world around us. The troubling issue is: Human beings can make sense of the world in inaccurate and corrupt ways.

In fact, the Bible explains that we all suffer from an inadequate understanding of the world: "For now we see in a mirror dimly, but then we will see face to face. Now I know only in part; then I will know fully, even as I have been fully known" (1 Cor. 13:12). If even the Apostle Paul admits to knowing "only in part," the same must be true for us all.

When humans communicate among one another and over the course of time, they tend to converge on interpretations of their world so much that they take certain "truths" for granted. Unfortunately, there are countless "truths" humans can take for granted as incontestable about the world, which, in fact, are not true. Imagine how many humans once believed the earth was flat. The "truth" was incontestable and common sense, but it was also nonetheless wrong. How do humans arrive at such inaccurate beliefs?: Those beliefs arise in their communication, which reinforce ideas time and time again in explicit and implicit ways.

Much of Jesus' ministry can be described as a confrontation with inaccurate beliefs, which were assumed true and incontestable because those inaccurate beliefs were reinforced in the everyday communication of his audiences. A major trouble with holding inaccurate beliefs is that they often encourage or invite certain behaviors, which naturally follow from those inaccurate beliefs. Picture, for example, how it "made sense" when infections were thought to come from tainted air (not bacteria and viruses) to reuse surgical instruments between patients without cleaning them to save time. In other words, our assumptions and expectations about how the world works shape our experiences and drive our behavior. That's a sophisticated idea but consider the following passage from the book of James:

> When we put bits into the mouths of horses to make them obey us, we can turn the whole animal, or take ships as an example. Although they are so large and are driven by strong winds, they are steered by a very small rudder wherever the pilot wants to go. Likewise, the tongue is a small part of the body, but it makes great boasts. Consider what a great forest is set on fire by a small spark. The tongue is also a fire, a world of evil among the parts of the body. It corrupts the whole person, sets the whole course of his life on fire, and is itself set on fire by hell (James 3:3-8).

Great teachers use metaphors to connect what we understand well with what we do not understand. Here, James knows that his audience will have difficulty grasping the idea that the tongue is powerful. To communicate that truth, he draws from what they already understand well: bits/horses, rudders/ships, and sparks/infernos. Of course, the equivalent relationship James is comparing to each of these at the end of this passage would be: communication/course of one's life. Each of these metaphors attempts to overcome the readers' beliefs about the significance of the tongue. In other words, James is confronting believers' taken-for-granted, but inaccurate, assumptions about communication—assumptions that ironically originate from their own way of talking. People tend to think that small inputs do not create big outputs. Horses, ships, and forest fires are majestic, powerful, and even awe-inspiring in good and bad ways. Picture for example the wonder of touching the sinews and shoulder muscles of a massive stallion or beholding a great forest fire approaching your home. James wants us to view the power of our talk with these same emotional reactions. Why? Because no less than "the whole course of . . . life" is determined therein.

How does that work? How does talk shape the trajectory of one's whole life? Part of the answer has to do with the idea that inaccurate beliefs—created when we give the wrong value or meaning to sin behavior repeatedly—encourages us, and others in our community, to keep sinning. James helps us on this point, by writing, "If any think they are religious, and do not bridle their tongue *but deceive their hearts*, their religion is worthless" (James 1:26). Look again: For James, controlling one's own speech is a matter of keeping the heart free from deception. Deception holds the idea that individuals are somewhat willful and at times complicit in taking up certain beliefs that fulfill lustful desire. Have you ever listened for what you wanted to hear? We all do, all the time. James writes:

> But *one is tempted by one's own desire*, being lured and enticed by it; then, when that desire has conceived, it gives birth to sin, and that sin, when it is fully grown, gives birth to death. Do not be deceived, my beloved (James 1:14-16).

Where beliefs are Godly, accurate, and reinforced in the community, sin is minimized because sin is no longer valued, praised, or deemed legitimate. Conversely, however, talk spreads wickedness from the individual to the community. Paul, providing advice and encouragement to a younger pastor named Timothy, also held the view that sinful talk is a cancer to be avoided. Paul wrote to Timothy:

> Avoid godless chatter, because those who indulge in it will become more and more ungodly, their teaching will spread like gangrene (NIV, 2 Tim 2:16).

We tend to think of chatter as insignificant, but Paul equates it to teaching and to gangrene. Chatter, gossip, and everyday talk are forms of teaching in the sense that they reinforce certain beliefs and teach us to hold views about what is valuable, disgusting, worthwhile, important, denigrating, beautiful, shameful, excellent, demeaning, positive, and cheap, among many others. Even the very topics we discuss in these informal settings—whether we know it or not—communicate through reinforcement what is *worth* discussing. Paul's use of the metaphor of gangrene highlights again how insidious sinful talk can be in the community. The same way gangrene spreads and deforms the physical body, godless talk spreads and deforms the body of Christ by distorting and corrupting beliefs, which in turn entices people to more sin. Paul makes that connection explicit by writing profane talk makes its participants "more and more ungodly" (2 Tim. 2:16). What kinds of talk encouraged your wrong beliefs, which, in turn, encouraged your sin?

From these passages, it appears that the Apostles had a picture of communication as a force of grave importance in the life of believers because communication invited beliefs that encouraged righteousness or wickedness in the community. Is it any wonder their view of communication led the Apostles to speak boldly against heresy and even led them to request that believers would pray that they speak with boldness against corrupt communication (compare with Eph. 6:19-20)? Paul characterized an aspect of his ministry as a kind of spiritual warfare in which the Apostles "*destroy arguments* and every proud obstacle raised up against the knowledge of God, and we take every thought captive to obey Christ" (2 Cor. 10:4-5). Again, God's plan for our communication should not be relegated to mere niceness and manners. Without question, politeness is a spiritual issue and charitable behavior toward others is of utmost importance to God (compare with 1 Cor. 13:13). However, that is not to say that argument has no place in Godly communication, especially when argument is used to confront error in belief systems that, if believed or assumed to be true, go on to encourage sinfulness.

---

## Discussion Questions, Chapter 3

1. Tell your story of a time when you held an inaccurate belief that you learned by your own or others' talk, which resulted in trouble.
2. According to James, how are our words akin to bits, rudders, and sparks? Why do you suppose James

needed to use so many metaphors to communicate his point?

3. Explain how communication is a special category of behavior. What does that tell you about the relationships among talk, behavior, and sin?

# CHAPTER 4

# **Talk that appears righteous can nonetheless be sinful**

In earlier chapters, I explained how a biblical understanding of Godly speech can be deeply complex because talk that might appear to be sinful (like engaging in confrontation and argumentation) can nonetheless be righteous, as with Jesus' words to the Pharisees in Matthew 12:33-36 and Paul's battle against heretics of the early church (see 2 Cor. 10). The story of God's plan for our communication gets even deeper because the opposite is also true: Talk that appears righteous can nonetheless be sinful.

Recall that Jesus' teaching helped us understand an expanded view of the Ten Commandments to include the role of talk in sin. As I described in a previous chapter, Jesus does this by discussing the commandments against murder (compare Ex.

20:13 and Mt. 6:21-22) and bearing false witness (compare Ex. 20:16 and Mt. 6:33-37). Consistent with these teachings, Jesus expands our view of the commandment to "Honor your father and mother" (Ex. 20:12 and Mt. 15:5) to include the role of talk in breaking the Law.

> Then the Pharisees and scribes came to Jesus from Jerusalem and said, "Why do your disciples break the tradition of the elders? For they do not wash their hands before they eat." He [Jesus] answered them, "And why do you break the commandment of God for the sake of your tradition? For God said, 'Honor your father and mother,' and, 'Whoever *speaks* evil of father and mother must surely die.' But *you say* that whoever tells father or mother, 'Whatever support you might have had from me is given to God,' then that person need not honor the father. So, for the sake of your tradition, you make void the word of God. You hypocrites" (Mt. 15:1-7)!

In this passage, Jesus confronts the Pharisees and scribes' teaching. Again, his confrontation of their wrong teaching includes language (i.e., You hypocrites!) that cannot be described as "nice." In fact, the disciples point out to Jesus that the "Pharisees took offense when they heard what you said" (Mt. 15:12). That observation continues to support the notion that talk that appears sinful can nonetheless be righteous—as Jesus was perfect and without sin (see 2

Cor. 5:21). Yet, in this passage, we see the opposite is also true: Talk that appears to be righteous can nonetheless be sinful. The Pharisees and scribes called on the authority of tradition to initiate a devious plot: They taught others to defraud their aging parents and avoid their duty to take care of them in old-age by invoking a very religiously-sounding justification (i.e., "Whatever support you might have had from me is given to God."). Whether this justification was a way of keeping money for oneself or was actually given to the Temple, God abhorred the practice on at least three accounts. Look closely at the preceding passage and you will see that Jesus is condemning (a) the practice of avoiding one's duty to parents, and (b) the talk used as a means of creating the appearance of justifying this obscene practice. Also, Jesus is condemning the Pharisees and scribes' (c) teaching others how to justify their sin using this religious-sounding talk. Such a teaching should make all teachers of the Scriptures swallow hard at the gravity of our task.

## Satan is the Great Deceiver

By now, I hope that you perceive how complex the issue of Godly communication can sometimes be. I am awestruck by how the Scriptures themselves communicate such complex lessons about communication. At this point, we have seen how talk is action and how talk can encourage beliefs that lead us to more sin or more righteousness (see Chapters 2 and 3, respectively). Furthermore, we have seen how some talk that appears to be sinful can in fact be righteous and how some talk that appears to be righteous can in fact be sinful (see Chapters 2 and 4, respectively).

Taken together, is it any wonder why Satan is referred to as the Great Deceiver? In Revelation 12:9 Satan is described as the "deceiver of the whole world." Elsewhere, Jesus describes Satan this way: "When he [Satan] lies, he speaks according to his own nature, for he is a liar and the father of lies" (Jn. 8:44). Recall that Satan's sophisticated deception tempted Adam and Eve (Gen. 3:1-5). Satan's deception spans human history and is part and parcel of his character and how he operates. Satan's deceptive nature is so pervasive, why wouldn't he also deceive us about talk? Talk is one of his primary weapons. It works to Satan's advantage for us to think little about and underestimate the power of talk in our spiritual lives and community.

---

## Discussion Questions, Chapter 4

1. Explain the following insight as a product of Satan's deception: Talk that appears wicked can nonetheless be righteous and talk that appears righteous can nonetheless be wicked.

2. What might be a modern-day version of the Pharisees' teaching, which invoked a religious-sounding justification for sin? Are religious leaders immune or especially vulnerable to ungodly speech of this sort? (see James 3:1-12)

3. What insights stand out to you about Chapters 1-4 as particularly surprising to you about the nature of Godly communication?

# CHAPTER 5

# You Say

In the first chapter, I explained how I undertook a close analysis of as many situations in the Bible as possible when God comments on our commenting. I wanted to find lessons or central themes. The task was arduous. Perceiving unifying themes was difficult, but the LORD provides. He is faithful to answer those who ask, seek, and knock (Mt. 7:7). Before I explain the results of my investigation, it is important to understand how communication is informational and in-formational.

## Communication is Informational and In-formational

Most everyone readily understands that communication is a means by which we transfer or transmit informational content. What is less obvious—although no less important—is that communication also forms the substance of identities and relationships in an ongoing manner. Strange idea? Consider this: I love my wife dearly and I am proud of our marriage relationship. Let's say I want to give our relationship a "high-five." Where do I go? Sure, I can give her a high-five, but she is an individual and does not represent the whole of our relationship. Our relationship, in a sense, exists at a different level of analysis than either of us as individuals. Our relationship is somehow "between" us—a state that cannot be reduced to its respective parts.

Consider, for example, how we cannot know the "wetness" of water by knowing all there is about hydrogen and oxygen. There is something uniquely special about *combination* in the social, physical, and, as we shall see, spiritual worlds. Communication is the place where that combination occurs in an ongoing manner. Communication is the actual location of identities and relationships. What is my marriage relationship, except for the aggregation of interactions between spouses? In speaking to my wife, I call into being our relationship—be it in healthy or unhealthy ways. Furthermore, it is in communication that I position my identity and hers. I could say, "Honey, would you help me remember my cell phone?" In doing so, I position her as my "Honey" and as someone who would or should "help me remember." Conversely, I position my identity as someone who has the moral right to call her "Honey" and as someone who needs help remembering. Our relationship and our respective identities are called into being in even these mundane, everyday situations of talk. Thus, as we speak, our relationships and identities are constantly "in-formation."

What's more, these relational and identity constructing features of talk are profoundly spiritual matters.

## Godly talk is humble, other-promoting, and God-fearing.

Understanding this dual-force of communication (i.e., information and "in-formation") is crucial to understanding what the many instances of "*You Say*" have in common. They each imply—in one way or another—that our language-use should be humble regarding ourselves, other-promoting in the fullest sense, and God-fearing. In nearly every instance where God comments on our speech, at least one of these lessons is at play. In other words, our communication should position others as more important and God as the authority of all. This idea is not new. Jesus explained:

> You shall love the LORD your God with all your heart, and with all your soul, and with all your mind. This is the greatest and first commandment. And a second is like it: You shall love your neighbor as yourself (Mt. 22:37-39).

I hope that the following analysis will reveal—in a new way—how integral the living-out of these commandments must be with how we approach our everyday talk. Among the more than one-hundred passages that begin with a variant of "you say" and constitutes God's commenting on our commenting, one text stands out as particularly apt at explaining the totality of this idea. The following is a close analysis of that biblical text, which illustrates all of these dynamics at the same time (i.e., Godly speech is humble, other-promoting, and God-fearing). In the following paragraphs, I explain that passage and how it relates to the results of my investigation.

## The Pharisees and the Canaanite Woman

In Matthew 15, Jesus has an encounter with the Pharisees and scribes in which they accuse him and the disciples of breaking the "tradition of the elders" for not washing their hands prior to eating (v. 1-2). As covered in a previous chapter, Jesus rebukes them strongly as hypocrites (v. 7) for teaching others that they can tell their aging parents, "Whatever support you might have had from me is given to God" (v. 5 compare with Mk. 7:11). In doing so, Jesus argued, the Pharisees were teaching people to break the fifth Commandment (Ex. 20:12). Immediately following this rebuke, Jesus "called the crowd to him and said to them, 'Listen and understand: It is not what goes into the mouth that defiles a person, but it is what comes out of the mouth that defiles'" (Mt. 15:10-11). Clearly, Jesus is highlighting the role of communication in the production and perpetuation of sin in the community. He admonishes us to "listen and understand" that *words* (i.e., what comes out of the mouth) *defile*. That is, the words we speak can make us spiritually unclean.

In these passages, Jesus is clearly attacking the accuracy of the informational aspect of the Pharisees and scribes' teaching, but he is also attacking the in-formational aspect of their communication as well. We might understand the Pharisees and scribes' message to parents as arrogant, other-harming, and God-using. Moreover, the Pharisees and scribes were teaching others to use language in like manner. We might diagram the in-formational aspect of their message to parents like this:

---

**Figure 1**

**The Sinful Teaching about Communication by the Pharisees in Mt. 15:5**

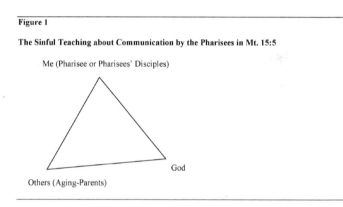

Me (Pharisee or Pharisees' Disciples)

God

Others (Aging-Parents)

---

Why? By *saying* (and teaching others to *say*), "Whatever support you might have had from me is given to God" the individual positions his identity as someone who can invoke the authority of God to avoid serving others. God is used as a kind of instrument or justification-source who parents must obey and who gets the individual a desired outcome of being free from moral duty. That is truly wicked speech, indeed!

Perhaps this idea will be clearer as we follow Jesus and his disciples further through this story: Soon after pronouncing to the crowd, "It is not what goes into the mouth that defiles a person, but it is what comes out of the mouth that defiles"

(v. 11), Peter asked Jesus to "Explain this parable to us" (v. 15). Here, Peter's words suggest how difficult it was for him to grasp that language-use could be a source of spiritual uncleanliness. He describes Jesus' words as a "parable." Parables are figurative and enigmatic stories that illustrate, but also obscure (see Mk. 4:10-12), a spiritual point.

Look again: "It is not what goes into the mouth that defiles a person, but it is what comes out of the mouth that defiles" (v. 11). Little about Jesus' words here resembles the figurative nature of a parable, with the minor exception that "mouth" is certainly used as a metaphor (*technically*, a synecdoche) for communication. In fact, Jesus seems to respond with frustration at Peter's description of his words as a parable. Jesus responds:

> Are you also still without understanding? Do you not see that whatever goes into the mouth enters the stomach, and goes out into the sewer? But what comes out of the mouth proceeds from the heart, and this is what defiles. For out of the heart come evil intentions, murder, adultery, fornication, theft, false witness, slander. These are what defile a person, but to eat with unwashed hands does not defile (Mt. 15:16-20).

Jesus responds to Peter by demonstrating just how literally, not figuratively, he intends for his teaching to be taken—going so far as to trace the digestive process from mouth to sewer in order to dispel the idea that he was in any way teaching that food is a source of defilement. Then, Jesus connects heart and mouth explicitly. Again, heart is used as a kind of metaphor to imply not the organ, but the aggregation of thoughts (Mt. 9:4), intentions (Heb. 4:12), emotions (Jn. 16:22), and conscience (Heb. 10:22). In other words, Jesus reveals a deep connection among thought-life, communication, and sin. He listed an extensive number of heinous sins. Look at them again. Do you really believe that sins like murder, fornication, and theft are deeply connected to communication? If not, Jesus' words have not yet penetrated your thinking about communication.

Importantly, Jesus is not necessarily emphasizing a linear sequence as much as the grave association among them. The association among thought-life, communication, and sin is not linear but cyclical and mutually constitutive. The Apostle James' teaching supports that notion. James writes, "If any think they are religious, *and do not bridle their tongues but deceive their hearts*, their religion is worthless" (James 1:26). Here, corruption (i.e., sin) in communication (i.e., "tongues") influences the thought-life (i.e., "hearts") such that sin is encouraged resulting in worthless religion (for more details, see Chapter 3).

## On to Tyre and Sidon

At this point in the narrative, Jesus attacked the Pharisees and scribes' communication and used it to teach the crowd and his disciples that communication, thought-life, and sin are thoroughly interconnected. When Peter was having difficulty understanding that message, the Bible records, "Jesus left that place and went to the district of Tyre and

Sidon" (v. 21). There, Jesus would meet a woman who would serve as the perfect object lesson for Godly communication in contrast with the religious—but thoroughly wicked—speech of the Pharisees and scribes. Jesus was the Great Teacher, indeed.

> Just then a Canaanite woman from that region came out and started shouting, "Have mercy on me, LORD, Son of David; my daughter is tormented by a demon." But he did not answer her at all. And his disciples came and urged him, saying, "Send her away, for she keeps shouting after us." He answered, "I was sent only to the lost sheep of the house of Israel." But she came and knelt before him, saying, "LORD, help me." He answered, "It is not fair to take the children's food and throw it to the dogs." She said, "Yes, LORD, yet even the dogs eat the crumbs that fall from the masters' table." Then Jesus answered her, "Woman, great is your faith! Let it be done for you as you wish." And her daughter was healed instantly" (Mt. 15:21-28).

Jesus' words must have been offensive to the woman. Jesus' comment, "It is not fair to take the children's food and throw it to the dogs (v. 26)" implies (a) the Jews, not the Canaanites, are the rightful recipients of his help and miracles, and (b) she is equivalent to a dog in terms of her value. Look carefully and you will see Jesus does not appear to be merely "nice" in his initial words to the Canaanite woman. The original Greek language includes a diminutive form in both Jesus' and the woman's words, making the translation closer to "little dog." In that sense, Jesus does seem to temper his words. However, the sting of his words cannot be reasoned away as merely the appearance of harshness. His words were harsh, but he was testing her and he knew her passing this test would be a marvelous lesson for his disciples (including us).

In the immediate moment after being the target of these offensive implications, the woman responds, "Yes, LORD, yet even the dogs eat the crumbs that fall from their masters' table." Wow. We need to think carefully about the other possibilities for her words in order to perceive just how amazing the woman's communication is. If someone implied that you do not deserve God's miracle as much as others and that you are equivalent to a puppy-dog, would you respond as the Canaanite woman did? I confess, I doubt I would react with the same spiritual fortitude the woman demonstrates.

Recall that early in the same chapter of Matthew, Jesus admonishes the Pharisees and scribes for teaching others *to say* to one's aging parents, "Whatever support you might have had from me is given to God" (Mt. 15:5). We illustrated how that communication is arrogant, other-harming, and God-using. In Jesus' quest to teach his disciples the important idea that "It is not what goes into the mouth that defiles a person, but it is what comes out of the mouth that defiles" (Mt. 15:11) and "What comes out of the mouth

35

proceeds from the heart" (Mt. 15:18) he leaves Gennesaret and the Pharisees (Mt. 14:34), taking his disciples to Tyre and Sidon (Mt. 15:21), knowing the Canaanite woman, and her Godly communication, will be there for them to hear. The Pharisees and scribes' communication positioned self as esteemed, others as not valued, and God as an instrument of the self's manipulation in-formationally.

Conversely, the Canaanite woman's words were humble, other-promoting, and God-fearing. Her communication positioned self as less valuable, others as more valuable, and God as above all. We might diagram the in-formational aspect of her message to Jesus like this:

---

**Figure 2**

**The *You Say* Model: The Canaanite Woman's Godly Speech in Mt. 15:27**

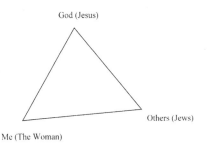

---

Why? By saying, "Yes, LORD, yet even the dogs eat the crumbs that fall from their masters' table" (v. 27) the woman takes up the lowly position into which Jesus placed her (i.e., as a little dog), and she recognizes that others are more valuable by not disagreeing that the Jews—not her—are the children in the metaphor. Finally, the woman is God-fearing, which is apparent in her first words (i.e., "Yes, LORD") as well as her willingness to take up and agree with the lowly and other-promoting positions into which Jesus was placing her. Clearly, Jesus was pleased with her communication. In fact, Mark's account makes that explicit. It reads, "Then, he [Jesus] said to her, "*For saying that*, you may go—the demon has left your daughter" (Mk. 7:29). Powerful. Oh, that Jesus might be that pleased with what we say.

My investigation of the instances in the Bible in which God (or Jesus) comments on our commenting rendered this model. As I mentioned earlier, I do not believe this idea is new (see Mt. 22:37), but, perhaps, it is a new way of thinking about what we already understood the Bible to be teaching us as it applies to our everyday communication. Many of the instances in which God comments on our commenting by including the phrase, "You say," in the Scriptures focus on only one aspect of this model. Yet, in another sense, to position any single identity of these associations between the self, others, and God's identity wrongly in our communication is to be wrong about every other identity. For me, Matthew 15 is the clearest and fullest explanation of Godly speech in the Bible that I have come to understand up to this point.

There are, however, literally more than a hundred more instances of "You say," which I have not yet covered. In the following chapters, I select more instances of "You say," as a means of illustrating and reviewing the importance of communicating in ways that are humble, other-promoting, and God-fearing.

---

## Discussion Questions, Chapter 5

1. Explain what is meant by the idea that communication is in-formational. What identities and relationships are being formed by the statement, "Only the weak-minded need God." Can you diagram it similar to the figures presented in this chapter? Be sure to distinguish the identities implied in this statement from the informational content of the statement.

2. Why do you suppose the disciples thought Jesus' teaching that "It is not what goes into the mouth that defiles a person, but it is what comes out of the mouth that defiles" (Mt. 15:11) was figurative and a parable? Discuss how you might help yourself understand Jesus' teachings about words are a literal reflection of spiritual conditions.

3. Discuss the Canaanite woman's words to Jesus. What are the other ways she could have responded? What makes her response such a powerful object lesson about Godly communication?

CHAPTER 6

# Zooming in: Godly speech is humble, not arrogant

So far we discussed important misconceptions about Godly communication as well as the general results of my investigation of the passages in the Bible in which God talks about our talk, triggered by the phrase, "You Say." In the previous chapter, I presented a model that demonstrates important and interrelated themes of these passages. Namely, these passages teach that Godly speech is humble, other-promoting, and God-fearing.

In the following three chapters, I provide more detail about each of the major components of the *You Say* model. In this particular chapter, I explore what it means for Godly speech to be humble and avoid arrogance. In the next chapter, I explore what it means for Godly speech to be other-promoting and avoid harming others. The chapter after that explores what it means for Godly speech to be God-fearing. In order to accomplish this explanation, I provide an Old and New Testament example in each of the following three chapters. I hope to "zoom in" on the three parts of the *You Say* model to give you a clearer picture of the many lessons the Bible teaches us about communication.

Before, I begin to explain the idea that Godly speech is humble in more detail, I wanted to emphasize again that the *You Say* model and its component parts (i.e., being humble, other-promoting, and God-fearing) are merely a summary of an extensive amount of study. This model is likely incomplete in the sense that no scholar can find the bottom of God's Word and there is always more to learn. Without question, there are a tremendous number of passages in the Bible that teach about communication. Let me give you a sense for what I mean. The topics addressed in these *You Say* passages vary widely. Consider just this abbreviated list of topics: gloating over others' pain (Ez. 35:10-15), saying others deserve punishment (Ez. 18:19), planning to defraud others (Deut. 15:9), saying there is no resurrection (1 Cor. 15:12), refusing to serve God (Jer. 2:12), refusing to hear God's correction (Am. 7:16), saying I am innocent of sin (Jer. 2:35-36), being confused by natural consequences of drunkenness (Prov. 23:35), saying I am hidden from God's accountability (Is. 29:15), saying God did not make us (Is. 29:16), saying God did not love us (Mal. 1:2), and saying I am safe because of my wealth (Rev. 3:17). In other words, a careful analysis of each of these situations recorded in the Bible could easily fill many volumes. In the name of brevity, however, I illustrate each of the three corners of the *You Say* model with an Old and New Testament example.

## An Old Testament Example

Let's first consider the idea that Godly speech is humble and not arrogant. What does such a teaching entail exactly? An important and repeated teaching regarding the nature of humble speech occurs in the pages of Deuteronomy. After God led Israel out of slavery in Egypt, God warned the people through Moses, "Do not exalt yourself, forgetting the LORD your God, who brought you out of the land of Egypt, out of the house of slavery" (Deut. 8:14). God goes on to say to them,

> Do *not say to yourself,* "My power and the might of my own hand have gotten me this wealth" (Deut. 8:17). . . . [and] Do *not say to yourself,* "It is because of my righteousness that the LORD has brought me in to occupy this land" (Duet. 9:4).

How tempting it is to attribute our wealth and successes to our own making. To speak of our station in life as the products of our own intellect, morality, and worth is inviting because it gives us a sense of self-satisfaction and the sense that we have immanent control over our lives. God blessed the nation of Israel by redeeming them from slavery and providing a wealthy land of inheritance. That process, however, unfolded over generations. How easy it is to look to our many inherited blessings and attribute those blessings to our own creation. In doing so, we further build up our ego by thinking or speaking that not only is life going well, but it is going well because I deserve for it to go well, or I earned my success without reference to the many advantages bestowed by God that made such success possible. In fact, without God's constant intervention in sustaining life itself such blessings would be impossible to enjoy in the first place. Without question, the Israelites fought battles, marched across deserts, and lived through difficult circumstances. The trouble is such hardships can become fodder for satanic influence in our thinking. Hardships can be easily reinterpreted as evidence of why blessings are now entitled to us or deserved. Can you relate? What difficulties or hardships have you endured, which could become fodder for giving sense to your current blessings as created by "the might of my own hand" or "because of my righteousness?"

Probably all of us can identify instances in our lives of when and where we had to sacrifice or endure hardship. However, in the passage above, God is warning against using those experiences as justifications for convincing ourselves that we now deserve, earned, or are entitled to blessing. In my own life, my wife and I endured the hardship of putting me through graduate school. I worked through years of higher education; how easy it is to speak like I now deserve the many blessings that have come from being a professor (see Chapter 1). These passages teach that I must remember that myriad forces outside of my control worked together to even allow me to attend school, much less graduate successfully. I could not enjoy my work and blessings that have flowed, if it were not for God's continual presence in allowing my heart to pump and my brain to function. The sum of these insights should lead me into a perpetual state of gratitude toward a God who blesses with unmerited favor.

Lest we forget, God wants to bless us (Ps. 37:4). He alone created pleasures and He promises we will have pleasures eternally in Heaven (Ps. 16:11). And yet, He is jealous for our relationship with Him (Ex. 34:14). A part of building that relationship is rightly recognizing the giver of the good gifts we enjoy (James 1:17).

Do you see how saying to yourself, "My power and the might of my own hand" and "It is because of my righteousness" invites sin in the sense that it inflates the idea of the self and the self's control over events? In both instances, speech is arrogant and it positions our identities as God-like. To believe and suggest in communication, "I made this success," is not Godly speech. To be sure, we *do not* have to have a low opinion of ourselves, but we need to be grateful to God for our successes. What success, what blessing, what wealth is possible without countless factors outside of our control—not the least of which being the very breath we breathe required to enjoy such blessings in the first place.

## A New Testament Example

Consider a related passage in the New Testament:

> Come now, *you who say*, "Today or tomorrow we will go to such and such a town and spend a year there, doing business

> and making money." Yet you do not even
> know what tomorrow will bring. What is
> your life? For you are a mist that appears for
> little while and then vanishes. Instead *you
> ought to say*, "If the LORD wishes, we will
> live and do this or that." As it is, you boast
> in your arrogance; all such boasting is evil
> (James 4:13-16).

Look again carefully at the contrast James creates between the wicked and righteous forms of communication. On close examination, you will see that the main difference is the addition of a single, minor clause: "If the LORD wishes." Clearly, James is not against business plans. Thinking about and planning for the future is wise (Prov. 21:5).

James is taking on a different aspect of speaking about the future that inflates the ego by making it seem like what we say about the future will come to pass. He is teaching believers not to be presumptuous in their speech about the location and source of ultimate control in this world.

In the first, wicked version of the message, the believer positions his identity as one who can make plans and implement them without reference to God. The arrogance of this positioning, embedded in the "in-formational" dimension of the message (see Chapter 4), is so subtle most of us would never become aware of it in our daily lives and talk. In other words, the phrases, "tomorrow we will go to . . . a town and spend a year there, doing business and making money," are a form of speech known as declaratives. Declaratives attempt to represent the factual state of affairs to others but they may not actually represent fact. Liars can, of course, use declaratives. Consider also the statement, "This page is white." My statement is declarative in that it makes an assertion and pronounces a truth. Of course, we can employ declaratives to make assertions that are not true or about matters that we have little understanding. I could write, "This book will be read by David Edwards." In doing so, I create an assertion, which may or may not be true because I do not know anyone named David Edwards. In much the same way, speaking about future business plans— or any plans for that matter—in declarative form, without reference to God, inflates the ego because it communicates to ourselves and others subtly that we can call the future into being with our words. Written differently, these kinds of messages position our identities as God-like.

You may recall from the first chapter how I came to be curious about the instances of "You Say" in the Bible: The Holy Spirit revealed to me how I failed to honor God with my words. We owned a house that just would not sell or rent, leaving us with two mortgage payments for ten months. I feel so silly in retrospect as I recall the times my wife and I discussed what we would do with the money we made on the property. We were spending the profits before we ever sold the house! We made plans that, on the face of it, appeared holy: 10% to the church and some set aside for friends who were struggling financially. What we never did, however, was stop to think—and speak—that the house will sell or rent, *if the LORD wills*. I confess I was arrogant in my speech. I like the way my wife explains it now: She explains that in our conversations about the house we were "training our brains," in subtle terms to view the future as a place where we had control and a place where God was a bystander. That kind of training-the-brain breeds sin.

Look again at the James passage. In the second, righteous version of the message, the believer positions his identity as one who can make plans and implement them, but only "if" power outside himself allows. Here, the declarative is transformed into the subjunctive. The subjunctive is a way to characterize some speech as concerned with some un-real state of affairs. For example, we might say, "If I can't make it home in time, we might need a different plan for dinner." In comments like this, the word, "if," allows us to use language to describe states of affairs in tentative and conservative ways, without making declarations about states of affairs we do not yet know for sure. In the example statement, the speaker communicates the possibility of making it home in time, while also describing the possibility of not making it home in time. That is the power of, "if."

Applied to James' teaching, he tells the believers to include the subjunctive phrase, "If the LORD wishes." In doing so, the believer includes the will of God as an important influence on a state of affairs, which are yet un-real and have yet to come to fruition. To include the phrase, "If the LORD wishes," is to position God's identity over the self, "in-formationally" (see Chapter 5). Is it any wonder why James includes the comments about the frailty and fleetingness of life between the first and second versions? He addresses how arrogant the declarative version of the believer's speech is before recommending believers use the subjective version.

Throughout the book of James, the Apostle takes issue with believers' communication. His teaching about communication even includes in this passage taking issue with the *absence of* reference to LORD. Again, the major difference between the first, wicked message and the second, righteous one is the addition of a few short words.

Can leaving out a few words really make that big of difference in the thought-life and sin of the believer and believing community? I believe that is exactly what James is teaching here, and that notion refocuses our attention on just how subtly our everyday talk can influence "the whole course of . . . life" (James 3:8). How? By positioning our identity as capable of determining our own future in our everyday talk—day after day and conversation after conversation—we come to believe that deception in our heart (compare with James 1:26). The inclusion or exclusion of these kinds of short phrases "trains our brains" and, in turn, creates expectations and assumptions that will lead us into more righteousness or more sin.

I would venture that for most believers, if asked directly, "Can you alone control and determine your life and future, or does God play an important role?" we would answer correctly. However, James is teaching how small word choices in our everyday talk corrupt our thinking. By declaring future plans without reference to the LORD we ignore His influence and position ourselves arrogantly. When the deceptive belief is ensconced, our judgment is corrupted.

Furthermore, by elevating the self, the need for others and God is diminished. That deceptive belief makes it much easier to harm others and ignore God. James is teaching that elevating the self can happen in everyday talk even by failing to acknowledge God's sovereignty over the future. In sum, these two passages—one from the Old Testament and one from the New Testament—are quite consistent in reference to the need for our speech to be humble.

---

## Discussion Questions, Chapter 6

1. Tell your story of a blessing that is tempting for you to attribute solely to your own efforts or qualities. How do these passages shape the way you should talk about those blessings?

2. What are some ways we talk about the future, which might lead us to position our own identity arrogantly?

3. How might the repetition of subtle but arrogant speech keep us from being other-promoting, charitable, and God-fearing?

# CHAPTER 7

# Zooming-in: Godly speech is other-promoting, not other-harming

In the previous chapter, we discussed the first of the three sides of the *You Say* model, and in this chapter, we discuss the second side: Godly speech is other-promoting, not other-harming. In the following paragraphs, I select two examples of passages that describe God's commenting on our commenting as it relates to others.

## An Old Testament Example

The prophet Ezekiel reported to Israel "The word of the LORD came to me" (Ez. 18:1). Apparently, a practice arose in Israel in which family members were being executed for the sins of other family members. What God spoke through Ezekiel illustrated His concern about a certain proverb or saying that sprang up and was being repeated in the community:

> What do you mean by repeating this proverb concerning the land of Israel, "The parents have eaten sour grapes, and the children's teeth are set on edge?" As I live, says the LORD God, this proverb shall no more be used by you in Israel. Know that all lives are mine (Ez. 18:2-4).

The worldly and secular proverb implies that there *should be* an interconnection between the sinful acts of parents and the judgment or consequences endured by their children. Notice, the LORD is offended not only by the content of the teaching, but that this wicked proverb is being "repeated" (Ez. 18:2). Later, in the same chapter of Ezekiel, the prophet admonishes that the LORD says to Israel:

> Yet *you say*, "Why should not the son suffer for the iniquity of the father?" When the son has done what is lawful and right, and has been careful to observe all my statutes, he shall surely live. The person who sins shall die (Ez. 18:19-20) . . . For I have no pleasure in the death of anyone, says the LORD (Ez. 18:32).

The secular proverb imbued the idea of harming others (in this case, family members of those who sinned) with a kind of moral force or support, making the sin of harming others a culturally-lauded platitude. Imagine how this proverb would come to be a part of the collective store of common sense when repeated over time and by leaders, bosses, parents, spouses, coworkers, cousins, and friends. But, of course, that common sense was corrupt. In turn, the actions that were justified by this erroneous common sense would be corrupt too. Imagine how innocent children were imprisoned, tortured, or killed for their parents' crimes— all the while such retribution and revenge was deemed legitimate by invoking such disgusting, albeit religiously-sounding, proverbs.

Are there worldly sayings or proverbs that we repeat? Yes. I encourage you to listen carefully for those one-liners that come up in your social world and that are used to justify behavior. A lesson we can take from Ezekiel is the need to test how such everyday proverbs align with God's wisdom. The Apostle John wrote, "Beloved, do not believe every spirit, but test the spirits to see whether they are from God" (1 John 4:1). I am convinced that some of the most insidious and worldly proverbs I have heard also tend to invoke the name of God. I think doing so adds a kind of moral force to the proverb and likely tricks some unwitting believers into thinking the proverb must therefore be Biblical. Consider these worldly and secular saying: "*God helps those who help themselves*" and "*God wants me to be happy.*" I include these in a section about how Godly speech is other-promoting, not other-harming because I have *only* heard these used in the context of justifying decisions that can hurt others. I have heard the first saying to justify lying and stealing and the second as a means of justifying divorce. Can you relate? What kinds of worldly sayings circulate in your everyday life that are used to justify harming others?

Let's be quick to follow the Apostle John's recommendation and test the spirits: Neither proverb is from the Bible, nor is their content similar to the spirit of Biblical teaching. In fact, if we were to make these proverbs similar in spirit to biblical teaching they should probably be something more like, "God helps those who help *His purposes*" (compare with Ps. 37:4) and "God wants me to be *holy*" (compare with 1 Peter 1:16). Do you see how much more difficult it would be to use these proverbs to justify harming others? Corrupt and worldly proverbs can trick—or lull—believers into a thought-life that invites sin.

## A New Testament Example

In the book of James, the Apostle admonished the young church to avoid making socio-economic status differentiations within their community, even though such distinctions were common of society outside the church.

> My brothers and sisters do you, with your acts of favoritism, really believe in our glorious LORD Jesus Christ? For if a person with gold rings and in fine clothes comes into your assembly, and if a poor person in dirty clothes also comes, and if you take

> notice of the one wearing the fine clothes
> *and say*, "Have a seat here, please," while to
> the one who is poor *you say*, "Stand there,"
> or "Sit at my feet," have you not made
> distinctions among yourselves, and become
> judges with evil thoughts (James 2:1-4)?

James contrasts the language directed to the wealthy churchgoer with that directed to the poor churchgoer. The language used with the wealthy attendee is polite and hospitable, while the language directed at the poor attendee is impolite and inhospitable. James is, of course, not condemning hospitality given to the wealthy attendee so much as he is condemning that a poor attendee is treated inhospitably because it is assumed the poor attendee is a less valuable addition to the community of believers. Prejudice motivated the believers' other-harming communication. Here, the believers' communication fails to be other-promoting in physical, social, and spiritual ways. Physically, commanding the poor attendee to stand without a seat is uncomfortable. Socially, commanding the poor attendee to sit at one's feet (as well as issuing the command itself) is symbolic of treating the attendee as an inferior or a subordinate. Spiritually, the combination of these inhospitable implications might dissuade the poor attendee from desiring to be a part of the family of God altogether.

For James, the observation of such corrupt communication among the believers leads him to question whether the Christians to whom he is writing, "*really believe* in our glorious LORD Jesus Christ" (James 2:1)? The issue is *that* important.

Notice too, how James connects the quality of their talk to the quality of their thoughts. Do you give the wealthy and those in powerful positions the benefit of the doubt? Do you hold your tongue more in their presence? Do you manage impressions with them and seek to benefit them to gain recognition and favor? The simple answer is, we all do. James is asking do you fail to be so other-promoting in your communication to those who are poor and who have no power to reward you? If so, it reveals just how evil our thoughts are in *both* scenarios. If we are kind to the powerful in order to receive reward, then we position others' identities as mattering only insofar as they can benefit us and not as intrinsically valuable without reference to us. If we are unkind to the un-powerful because no reward is likely, then we position others' identities as not intrinsically valuable since they cannot benefit us. Everyday speech practices—like being polite to powerful others and not to those who have no power—can distort and corrupt our thought-life and encourages sins, especially those sins involving defrauding others (e.g., adultery, theft, and false witness) because such prejudice and differentiations in everyday talk treat others as important on the grounds of their transactional potential.

The process might unfold like this: We size people up for how much we can likely get out of them and then communicate with them accordingly. To the powerful, wealthy, and influential, we pander. To the weak, poor, and lonely, we are terse. The trouble is, those reactions "train our brains" to interact with others on the basis of what we can potentially receive from them rather than as worthy creations of God in their own right.

Others are valuable to God and he asks us to demonstrate our love for Him through our love for others (Mt. 22:39). Have you ever considered how being impolite and inhospitable to those who might be deemed your subordinate or inferior in society can create conditions that encourage sin? Have you ever considered how being polite and hospitable to those who might be deemed your supervisor or superior in society—only because of their ability to reward you—can create the conditions that encourage sin? In sum, these two passages—one from the Old Testament and one from the New Testament—are quite consistent in reference to the need for our speech to be other-promoting.

---

## Discussion Questions, Chapter 7

1. List some cultural and secular sayings that come up in the media or your workplace. How could such sayings train your own and others' brains for defrauding others?

2. Do you find it difficult to be polite and hospitable to the poor, aging, ailing, or indigent? Is it as easy to be mindful of your impressions with the homeless as with your boss? Why?

3. Tell your story a time when you were positioned as esteemed by someone who you expected to demean you. How did it make you feel? How can you practice similar acts of graciousness in your speech?

# CHAPTER 8

# Zooming-in: Godly Speech is God-fearing

In the previous two chapters, we discussed the first two of three sides of the *You Say* model. In this chapter, we discuss the last side: Godly speech is God-fearing. In the following paragraphs, I select two examples of passages that describe God's commenting on our commenting as it relates to Himself.

## An Old Testament Example

The prophet Isaiah spoke to Israel, who often prophesied about coming judgment. In one such prophesy, Isaiah reports God's words to be:

> The LORD said: Because these people draw near with *their mouths and honor me with*

*their lips*, while their hearts are far from me, and their worship of me is a human commandment learned by rote; so I will again do amazing things with this people, shocking and amazing. The wisdom of their wise shall perish, and the discernment of the discerning shall be hidden. Ha! You who hide a plan too deep for the LORD, whose deeds are in the dark, and *who say*, "Who sees us? Who knows us?" You turn things upside down! Shall the potter be regarded as the clay? Shall the thing made *say* of its maker, "He did not make me;" or the thing formed *say* of the one who formed it, "He has no understanding" (Is. 29:13-16)?

The people's communication offended the LORD, in part, because of the mindless and ritualistic nature of their words in worship that are uttered alongside comments that denote doubt in His existence, His knowledge, and His power to judge their sins. The honor given in words of sacred worship is juxtaposed against dishonor given in everyday, secular talk. The passage gives us the sense that dishonor directed to God in the talk of everyday life is bad, but, when contextualized by hollow words of honor, those dishonoring words become especially disrespectful. I can imagine times in my life when I worshiped God on Sunday but spoke with irreverence among friends on Friday. Perhaps you can recall doing the same? The presence of *both* kinds of talk from the same speaker produces a divided relationship with God. From this passage, we get the idea that followers of God were moving back and forth from confessing the authority of God to doubting and disparaging the authority of God without being convicted of the problematic duplicity such opposite words and thought-lives create. This duplicity of speech is an especially insidious state for believers because it allows them to practice *in*authenticity in their reverence toward God. When such talk fails to be genuinely God-fearing and is practiced week after week, a luke-warmness (Rev. 3:16) of affection for God is sure to take hold and be difficult to unstop. Of course, it is hard to know when duplicity has ceased because duplicity is deception.

Notice also that the passage directs believers' attention to how their words position their identities relative to God's identity inappropriately: "You turn things upside down! Shall the potter be regarded as the clay . . ." (Isa. 29:16). For me, I picture the *You Say* model being turned upside down, much like how I characterized the speech of the Pharisees in Chapter 5. The believers' duplicity, in this Isaiah passage, demonstrated how they did not take seriously God's authority. They were God-fearing in hollow words at worship, but were irreverent in discussing their sins at all other times. In what ways are your words duplicitous between worship and the workweek?

## A New Testament Example

Jesus points out another pattern of duplicity in regards to believers' apparent, but not actual, reverence for God in their words.

> He also said to the crowds, "When you see a cloud rising in the west, *you immediately say*, 'It is going to rain;' and so it happens. And when you see the south wind blowing, *you say*, "There will be scorching heat;' and it happens. You hypocrites! You know how to interpret the appearance of earth and sky, but why do you not know how to interpret the present time (Luke 12:54-56)?

The people of Palestine in Jesus' day depended on the weather for survival and therefore became quite concerned and involved with accumulating a discriminatory and detailed understanding of natural forces. They studied the patterns of weather and its effects on agriculture; their bellies and lives depended on it. Jesus contrasts their eagerness to obtain this deep understanding of the material world with their unwillingness to develop a similarly deep understanding of the spiritual world—despite the fact that it mattered to their very souls and that they had ample means of cultivating a deep understanding. Here, Jesus is not condemning their words about the weather as much as he is using those words to contrast with their words about learning about God.

We live in a truly unique time. Today, seventh graders are taught facts about their physical world that would have utterly amazed the ancient people of Palestine. Consider the wonder of the periodic table—a systematic characterization of all known elements and their essential atomic makeup. To the ancient peoples, such knowledge would have been unimaginable. Think also how in the age of social media, gossip magazines, and entertainment television we know so much about and devote study to celebrities and their romantic relationship troubles. Many hours a day could be spent—and indeed are spent—learning about the love lives of strangers.

Yet, despite all our study and understanding of the physical world and lives of celebrities, biblical illiteracy is the norm. In the passage above, Jesus is using a "you say" to contrast their sophisticated predictions and analyses of the material world with their espoused and enacted ignorance of the spiritual world. He calls them "hypocrites" because their sophisticated understanding of the weather reveals the mask they wear to avoid obtaining a deeper understanding of God.

You can picture believers and nonbelievers—both then and today—saying of God and faith, "Faith is fine up to a point." These kinds of statements keep God at arm's length. These declarations of desired ignorance about God could even take on a holy or intellectual-sounding quality as in, "We can't possibly know what God wants from us," or "If god is really God, why would He bother with us?" Those words fail to be God-fearing because God has provided ample revelation—both general (Ps. 16:1-4; Rom. 1:20) and special (Heb. 4:12; 2 Tim. 4:16-17)—for us to cultivate a relationship with Him, if we are only willing to do so.

The truth is, many would rather not know more about God, because they have the hunch (correctly) that a deeper knowledge of Him would necessarily require them to submit their will to His (see Rom. 1:28-36). In doing so, they would have to position God's identity above their own.

Here again, Jesus is pointing out that those in the audience *speak* with clarity and keen discernment about some subjects, while avoiding or claiming ignorance on the most important subject of God. The *presence* of clear speech about the physical world and the *absence* of clear speech about God are labeled by Jesus as hypocrisy. Think even deeper with me: If day after day a person speaks sophisticatedly about the world around them, while avoiding or ignoring the subject of God, that state of affairs may reinforce for the individual the following illogical conclusion: "Since I know *so much about so much*, and I do not know much about God, it is probably because there is not much to know."

Again, communication trains our brains, both for good and ill. Surely, many educated and learned persons are tempted by their own words in this way. Jesus' teaching in this passage reminds us the importance of including thoughtful and thorough discussions of God in our intellectual pursuits. In doing so, we remain God-fearing in the sense that when we include such discussions we imply the worthiness and value of knowing more about God. In sum, these two passages—one from the Old Testament and one from the New Testament—are quite consistent in reference to the need for our speech to be God-fearing.

## Discussion Questions, Chapter 8

1.  Tell your story of a time you were reverent in one setting but irreverent in another. How do such divisions train your brain?

2.  What are some ways we talk about God, which might lead us to position our own identity arrogantly?

3.  How might sophisticated discussions and studies of topics—from chemistry to celebrities—*in the absence* of investigations of God undermine the truth that God is knowable and wants a personal relationship with us?

CHAPTER 9

# "You Say" in the Parable of the Prodigal Son

In the preceding Chapters, I advanced the idea that Godly communication positions the identities of the self, others, and God in appropriate ways, while sinful communication fails to position those identities appropriately. Metaphorically and diagrammatically, we can think of a triangle set askew in which the self is slightly lower than others and God is above both the self and others (see Chapter 5 for a detailed explanation). Communication that fails to position identities in these ways creates the conditions in which sin festers. In the following paragraph, I provide one more dramatic example of this idea by analyzing some of the dialogue presented in the Parable of the Prodigal Son.

The Gospel of Luke records the following story, told by Jesus.

> Then Jesus said, "There was a man who had two sons. The younger of them *said to his father,* 'Father, give me the share of the property that will belong to me.' So he divided his property between them. A few days later the younger son gathered all he had and traveled to a distant country, and there he squandered his property in dissolute living. When he had spent everything, a severe famine took place throughout that country, and he began to be in need. So he went and hired himself out to one of the citizens of that country, who sent him to his fields to feed the pigs. He would gladly have filled himself with the pods that the pigs were eating; and no one gave him anything. *But when he came to himself he said,* "How many of my father's hired hands have bread enough to spare, but here I am dying of hunger! I will get up and go to my father, and *I will say to him*, 'Father, I have sinned against heaven and before you; I am no longer worthy to be called your son; treat me like one of your hired hands.'" So he set off and went to his father. But while he was still far off, his father saw him and was filled with compassion; he ran and put his arms around him and kissed him. *Then*

*the son said to him*, "Father, I have sinned against heaven and before you; I am no longer worthy to be called your son." But the father said to his slaves, 'Quickly, bring out a robe—the best one—and put it on him; put a ring on his finger and sandals on his feet. And get the fatted calf and kill it, and let us eat and celebrate; for this son of mine was dead and is alive again; he was lost and is found!' And they began to celebrate. Now his elder son was in the field; and when he came and approached the house, he heard music and dancing. He called one of the slaves and asked what was going on. He replied, "Your brother has come, and your father has killed the fatted calf, because he has got him back safe and sound." Then he became angry and refused to go in. His father came out and began to plead with him. *But he answered his father*, "Listen! For all these years I have been working like a slave for you, and I have never disobeyed your command; yet you have never given me even a young goat so that I might celebrate with my fiends. But when this son of yours came back, who has devoured your property with prostitutes, you killed the fatted calf for him!" Then the father said to him, "Son, you are always with me, and all that is mine is yours. But we had to celebrate and rejoice, because this

> brother of yours was dead and has come to
> life; he was lost and has been found" (Luke
> 15:11-32).

For our purposes, we can think of the dialogue of the story turning at three key points: (a) the younger son's offensive request of the father, (b) the younger son's words to himself, and subsequent apology to his father, and (c) the older brother's offensive words to the father about both the father and his brother. Importantly, this story is a parable meant to represent our relationships with God (played by the role of the father) and one another (played by the brothers). In the following paragraphs, I hope to show how the story can be read as portraying archetypal models of Godly communication and unrighteous communication.

At the beginning of the parable, the younger son requests his inheritance from his father and implies he wishes his father were deceased (the regular time at which inheritances are dispersed). The son's words position his identity in relationship to the father. Specifically, his words imply an unwillingness to recognize his father as an authority. In that sense, his words are unrighteous because they fail to position the father's authority as rightful and fail to submit humbly to that authority.

In the middle of the parable, the younger son wises up and discovers that being under the father's authority—despite that it requires his humility—is a *desirable* state of affairs. The younger son goes so far as to practice his speech to his father—a speech that realigns his previous unrighteous positioning of identities with a righteous one. In fact, his apology to his father (a communicative act that necessarily positions the self humbly) includes a further deprecation of his identity in relationship with the father ("I am no longer worthy to be called your son;" Lk. 15:21). His message is a model of Godly communication. When we address God, we must be humble and God-fearing. We must willingly position our identity as lowly and His identity as worthy of authority and glory.

Toward the conclusion of the parable, the older son praises himself, denigrates the father for his decision to receive back his son without retribution, and disparages his younger brother for his earlier decision-making. The older brothers' words praise his own righteousness ("I have been working like a slave, and I have never disobeyed your command" Lk. 15:29). In doing so, he positions his identity in arrogant ways, but he also positions his father's identity as unjust for treating him like a "slave." That theme continues as the older son includes the words, "You have never given me even a young goat" (Lk. 15:29). The older brother then characterizes *his* younger brother as "this son of *yours*" (Lk. 15:30) and describes him as devouring property and cavorting with prostitutes. The net effect of the identity positioning accomplished by his words reveals his thought-life in which he sees himself as worthy, others as unworthy, and the father as an unjust power unworthy of the authority he holds.

The parable is full of lessons. For our purposes though, I want to direct your attention to the fact that the older brother *appears* to be living righteously, especially in comparison to his younger brother. The older brother continues to work for his father, while his brother shows contempt for the father in asking for his inheritance early. Yet, the end of the parable reveals that the older brother likely felt contempt for his father and brother throughout these unfolding events. The older brother's words reveal a disdain for the father as well as his brother and indicate a thought-life in which he conceived of himself as the only righteous and deserving member of the family. Is it any wonder he would react as he did to his father and brother?

---

## Discussion Questions, Chapter 9

1. Looking again at how each of the brothers addresses the father at the beginning and end of the parable, which messages are you more likely to identify with? Why?

2. Speculate how the older brother's communication to others about his brother and father might have trained his brain to create pride and contempt.

3. In what ways, are you now able to understand *the role of communication* in this parable, which were not apparent to you prior to reading this chapter?

CHAPTER 10

# The Practices of Godly Communication

The preceding chapters reveal that God's plan for communication is richly complex, but, from another view, it is simple in its profundity. There are an incomprehensible number of topics we can discuss with the content of our words. As we have seen, the Bible provides advice about a huge variety of communication circumstances (see the beginning of Chapter 6). However, a unifying theme of these passages suggests that Godly communication will always at its core position our identity in relationship to others and God in ways that please Him (see Chapters 6-9). Conversely, communication that God abhors fails to position our own identity in relation to others and God in ways that demonstrate humility about ourselves, love of others, or reverence to Him. In the following paragraphs, I explain another recurring theme of Godly communication presented in the New Testament: Godly speech gives grace to others and gratitude to the LORD.

## Godly speech gives grace to others.

Paul provided much advice about how to live out a faith in God in one's speech. He implored the Colossians to, "Let your speech always be *gracious*, seasoned with salt, so that you may know how you ought to answer everyone" (Col. 4:6). Because there are so many and varied issues and tasks we take up with our words in everyday talk, I am glad to have advice, which helps me, "know how . . . to answer everyone." Paul teaches that the central standard for our words is grace. The Greek word for grace is virtually synonymous with charity or charitable. Charity is giving goodness to those who need it and epitomizes the love that God gives humankind through the sacrifice of His son, Jesus Christ. When we receive charity from others (i.e., getting goodness from others), we cannot help but feel a sense of gratitude and a desire to express that gratitude to the source of charity. In that sense, grace and gratitude are two sides of the same coin.

Again, notice how, if the standard is to be gracious by giving goodness to others, our speech will be other-promoting inherently. That is not to say, we must be merely "nice." Being gracious and charitable is other-promoting because it is oriented toward supplying others' *needs*. Sometimes, genuine graciousness takes the form of truth-telling— including the truth that the other is in error—and could, therefore, on the face of it, appear to lack the quality of affirming the other (compare with Jesus' use of "brood of vipers" in Mt. 12:34, Chapter 3). Consider Paul's advice to the Colossians: "Let the word of Christ dwell in you richly; *teach and admonish one another in all wisdom*" (Col. 3:16). This advice implies that some Godly speech includes admonitions, but, of course, such moral instruction is to be done with "all wisdom." A sincere concern for other believers may require us to address their error and teach; however, such communication must be tempered by an authentic inspection of our heart and how our moral instruction positions the identity of the other. Jesus was regularly furious with so-called moral instruction that used God as a pretext for defrauding others (see Mt. 15:1-9, and Chapter 5). In such a scenario, the *appearance* of moral instruction can actually position one's identity as more valuable or esteemed than others, and God as an instrument of our own direction.

How is gracious speech accomplished? Since we understand that the word, "gracious," is associated with the idea of charity, how can we make our speech charitable? One way is to resist the constant temptation to hold others to a higher standard than we hold ourselves. How common is it to attribute others' behavior to shortcomings in their character, while we attribute similar behaviors in ourselves to mere external forces? Imagine, for example, the everyday scenario in which your spouse is running late for a dinner. How easy and tempting it is to think of your spouse as chronically irresponsible, when, if you ran late, you would rarely, if ever, consider labeling yourself the same way. In fact, most of us would have a long list of external reasons why we were late: traffic, annoying bosses, broken watches, long-winded clients, and long lines in the grocery checkout. Furthermore, we would almost certainly restrict our consideration of being late to the particular instance in question, without reference to any pattern in our behavior across time.

In the same way, we are called to be as charitable in attributing meaning to and labeling others' behavior as we are to ourselves. Here again, we see the intimate interconnection between thought-life, communication, and sin, which Jesus described (see Mt. 15:16-20, and Chapter 5). If we attribute chronic irresponsibility to our spouse and accept that kind of thinking uncritically, those thoughts will invite us to be rude, inconsiderate, and seek justice by attempting to correct our spouse's behavior in our communication with them. Over time, uncharitable messages will be exchanged between spouses who suffer from uncharitable thinking about one another. The situation is a breeding ground for sins like lying, adultery, and coveting of others' spouses (Ex. 20:17). The temptation and tendency to be uncharitable in our thinking and speech is so pervasive that for those reading these words it may be easier to "understand" how your spouse is "more" guilty of such ungraciousness than the reader—which is, of course, evidence of the very lesson I am describing. After explaining this dynamic to a group of college students one day, a young woman in the audience raised her hand. She explained confidently, "I don't do that." To which I responded, "Exactly." Left to our own devices, we will be charitable to ourselves. Let us pray that the LORD would grow within us the ability to be charitable to those He loves—those all around us (Luke 10:25-37).

Paul wrote to the Ephesians, "Let no evil talk come out of your mouths, but only what is useful for building up as there is need, *so that your words may give grace to those who hear*" (Eph. 4:29). Godly speech is other-promoting by being gracious and charitable, word-by-word and conversation-by-conversation.

## Godly speech gives gratitude to God.

The call to being gracious in our communication with others is a difficult one. Being charitable requires vigilance in inspecting one's own thought-life and everyday talk. Why do we take on such a challenge? In a word: gratitude. A unifying theme of the New Testament's description of Godly speech includes a recurring teaching that Christians are to praise and thank God. When we thank God, we position His identity—and our own in relationship to Him—rightly. To thank is to recognize another's influence and honor that influence. The writer of Hebrews explained, "And without faith, it is impossible to please God, for whoever would approach him must believe that he exists and that he rewards those who seek him" (Heb. 11:6). Thanking God affirms implicitly a belief in His existence and honors His existence as a rewarding force in our lives.

Consider the following passages: Paul wrote to early believers imploring them that they should be, "*giving thanks* to God the Father at all times and for everything in the name of our LORD Jesus Christ" (Eph. 5: 20), to "*Be thankful.* Let the word of Christ dwell in you richly; teach and admonish one another in all wisdom; and *with gratitude in your hearts* sing psalms, hymns, and spiritual songs to God" (Col. 3:15-16), and to "*Rejoice* always. Pray without ceasing, and *give thanks* in all circumstances; for this is the will of God in Christ Jesus for you. Do not quench the Spirit" (1 Thes. 5:16-19). Clearly, gratitude is an important feature of Godly communication. In the last passage, Paul seems to equate the giving of thanks to God with perpetuating the Spirit's presence in one's life.

Likewise, Paul taught the Philippian church:

> *Rejoice* in the LORD always; again I will say, '*Rejoice.*' Let your gentleness be known to everyone. The LORD is near. Do not worry about anything, but in everything, by prayer and supplication *with thanksgiving* let your requests be made known to God. And the peace of God, which surpasses all understanding, will guard your hearts and your minds in Christ Jesus (Phil. 4:4-7).

Rejoicing in the LORD is akin to speaking with gratitude that He exists and that His presence represents a positive influence in your life. Look again, at this famous passage, did you notice how the rejoicing and giving thanks to God in our speech is connected to the state of our hearts and minds? Paul writes that "the peace of God" in the heart and mind emerges, in part, from our rejoicing and giving of thanksgiving in our speech. What we say shapes what we think and vice versa. Want to protect your heart and mind? One way to start is to rejoice in the LORD. Again, I say, "Rejoice!"

## Discussion Questions, Chapter 10

1. How might giving grace to others be related to giving gratitude to God?
2. Tell the story of a time you found yourself tempted to attribute an uncharitable interpretation to a friend or family members' action. How did the uncharitable interpretation influence your communication with them? How did it influence your relationship with them? How did you overcome the uncharitable interpretation?
3. What three things can you praise God for right now?

# Who Do *You Say* I Am?

The most God-honoring form of communication is to recognize Jesus is the Christ, the son of the Living God. Matthew records:

> Now when Jesus came into the district of Caesarea Philippi, he asked his disciples, "Who do people say that the Son of Man is?" And they said, "Some say John the Baptist, but others Elijah, and still others Jeremiah or one of the prophets." He said to them, "But who do *you say* that I am?" Simon Peter answered, "You are the Messiah, the Son of the Living God." And Jesus answered him, "Blessed are you, Simon son of Jonah! For flesh and blood has not revealed this to you, you are Peter, and on this rock I will build

my church, and the gates of Hades will not
prevail against it" (Mt. 16:13-18)

Jesus built His church on this singular instance of Godly communication. So powerful was this communication, that Jesus promised death itself would not be able to overcome its life-giving consequences. So, how about you? Who do *you say* He is?

# ABOUT THE AUTHOR

Ryan Bisel (Ph.D., University of Kansas) is an associate professor of communication at the University of Oklahoma. Bisel is a researcher, author, consultant, and teacher in the areas of behavioral ethics and organizational communication. Bisel and his wife have two children and enjoy co-leading a community group of young families at their local church.

Printed in the United States
By Bookmasters